LOST LINES OF ENGLAND
BIRMINGHAM TO WORCESTER

ROGER NORFOLK

GRAFFEG

CONTENTS

Foreword	3
Introduction	4
Birmingham Snow Hill	13
Handsworth & Smethwick	23
Smethwick Junction	26
Old Hill	31
Stourbridge Junction	35
Kidderminster	42
Hartlebury	51
Droitwich Spa	53
Worcester Shrub Hill	58

FOREWORD

The Birmingham Snow Hill to Worcester Shrub Hill route escaped the mass closures of the 1960s. Whilst towns like Halesowen, Brierley Hill, Dudley, Bewdley and Stourport-on-Severn saw their rail services removed, the Worcester line remained to serve Stourbridge, Kidderminster, Droitwich Spa and communities in between. But the importance of such towns to the local and national economy was not immediately apparent to early railway builders.

The area to the west of Birmingham that included the myriad of industries within the Black Country was initially missed. To its east, interest was to have a direct route from Birmingham to the docks at Gloucester and Bristol. To its north, the Great Western Railway was working to complete their Wolverhampton to Birmingham line to give direct access to London. To its south and west came a line from Oxford through Worcester to give northward connections at Wolverhampton.

Only with the successful completion of these railways did attention turn to tapping into the considerable trade possible within Black Country communities between Stourbridge and Birmingham. The canal system had been their dominant transport route, but now the railway would add an extra dimension. This densely populated area of housing and industry would become criss-crossed with tracks for transporting raw materials and the goods they produced.

This book charts the development of the Snow Hill to Worcester route through its various building phases, with photographs showing a selection of its trains and services up to the last steam workings in 1966. In more recent times, the Snow Hill link was closed and removed, but its rebuilding has given enhanced travel opportunities. The route is again an important contributor to the West Midlands passenger transport network.

INTRODUCTION

The Black Country boundaries are not easily defined. On this Birmingham to Worcester route the area between Smethwick and Stourbridge approximately follows its southern edge, but it then extends northwards through West Bromwich and Dudley as far as parts of Walsall and Wolverhampton. It is an area of the West Midlands long known for its rich variety of raw materials. Natural resources of coal, limestone and iron ore gave rise to a basic iron smelting industry as early as the Middle Ages, and techniques developed in the 17th century by the Ward family of Dudley Castle, later the Earls of Dudley, helped pave the way to the Industrial Revolution. Increasing industrialisation gave rise to canals as an efficient transport system but by the early 19th century news of a developing rail alternative was spreading. The Wards owned mines at Pensnett and decided to lay a three-mile line, the Kingswinford or Shutt End Railway, to transport coal to a canal basin at Ashwood. To work on this railway, Foster, Rastrick & Co. of Stourbridge supplied an 0-4-0 tender locomotive, *Agenoria*, in 1829. Working successfully for many years, she was subsequently presented to the Science Museum in 1885 and is now in the collection of the National Railway Museum in York. A sister locomotive, *Stourbridge Lion*, was built at the same time for the Delaware & Hudson Canal Company in the USA, where she became the first locomotive to be steamed on that continent. Unfortunately, problems arose and she was laid up and partially dismantled, but what remains also survives. Through the KR and these locomotives, the Stourbridge area was an early contributor to railway development.

The Earl of Dudley continued to develop his railway system through the Pensnett Railway, constructed to supply his Round Oak ironworks and later absorbing the KR. This was always a purely industrial system although it later connected with the main line. Other bodies proposed various schemes for public railways to connect Birmingham and/or Wolverhampton with towns such as Dudley, Halesowen, Stourbridge, Kidderminster and further afield, but these were not supported. The first railway that came close was the Birmingham & Gloucester Railway in 1840, which descended the Midlands plateau by the steep two-mile Lickey Incline to Bromsgrove and then headed directly via Cheltenham to Gloucester for the docks. This did not serve the towns mentioned previously, but Worcester and Droitwich were not completely forgotten, as each had a road connection to stations on the line, Worcester to Spetchley and Droitwich to Droitwich Road.

Towns between Stourbridge and Worcester were placed onto the railway map by the Oxford, Worcester & Wolverhampton Railway, which received Royal assent on 4th August 1845. This was a line from Oxford, through the Cotswold Hills to Worcester, which then continued northwards through Stourbridge and Dudley to connect with the Grand Junction Railway at Wolverhampton. However, building this was not to be an easy ride. Steering between its directors' interests, railway politics and the raising of finances proved a difficult path, and it was seven years before rails connected local towns in the West Midlands and 1854 before the whole line opened as intended.

Wolverhampton was the OWW's destination of choice for several factors. Trade would be generated by towns like Stourbridge and Kidderminster and connection with the GJR at Wolverhampton provided a route to and from northwestern towns and cities. However, in return, the GJR had designs on a London route that bypassed the London & Birmingham Railway, with whom they shared facilities in Birmingham but did not have the best relations. At Oxford, the OWW was to connect with the Great Western Railway, who also agreed to lease the line for 999 years. GWR's Brunel surveyed the proposed line, gave his estimate for construction and became its engineer. However, to accommodate both the GJR and GWR railways' interests, the whole line would be constructed in mixed gauge.

By 1847 and with money running low, building the Evesham – Worcester – Wolverhampton section was suspended to concentrate southwards. Work here also eventually ceased, and it looked as if there was a possibility of the whole project being abandoned. Affected towns sent representatives to the Attorney General, and the Board of Trade invoked a clause in the 1845 Act to order the GWR to complete the line. However, this fell on deaf ears, as they were too busy elsewhere, but, fortunately, the OWW found more money and work restarted. In fact, the Midland Railway, of which the B&G was now part, had already built the section southwards from Worcester to connect with its line at Abbotswood Junction, so Worcester was already on the railway map from October 1850.

Meanwhile, the OWW had taken some decisions about junctions around Wolverhampton. By now, the GJR and L&B had patched up their differences to become constituents of the London & North Western Railway. The original connection with this line at Bushbury was still planned but other junctions were added, both at Priestfield with the Birmingham, Wolverhampton & Dudley Railway and at Tipton with the LNWR line between Birmingham and Wolverhampton. The BW&DR was a mixed-gauge line under construction that would become part of the GWR main line to London Paddington,

On 18th February 1852 the OWW opened between Worcester and Droitwich and continued via a link to the MR at Stoke Works Junction, south of Bromsgrove. This completed a loop to enable the MR to run some of their Bristol, Gloucester and Birmingham trains via Worcester without reversal. Two months later, the OWW was complete for trains to run between Worcester and Stourbridge. To provide a depot and repair works for the company's rolling stock, land was purchased at Worcester to build the necessary facilities. With two companies now using the station, Worcester Shrub Hill became jointly run, this situation continuing until railway nationalisation in 1948. From there, the OWW line in both directions was completed in stages, although this was not without further controversy and legal proceedings. The original Act stipulated that the line must be laid in mixed gauge but the OWW, clearly not intending to run broad-gauge trains, had laid parts only in standard gauge. Upon final inspection, the officer insisted the Act's clauses be honoured and only his successful running of a broad-gauge train throughout between Oxford and Wolverhampton satisfied his requirements.

There were now factions within the OWW boardroom, with some directors insisting a link be built north of Oxford between the OWW and a branch of the LNWR serving Oxford from Bletchley. Construction was authorised and through trains ran between Wolverhampton and London Euston from April 1854. However, these only lasted until 1861, when the OWW was absorbed into the GWR, who promptly curtailed the Euston service in favour of their Paddington terminus.

By the late 1850s, the OWW was looking for expansion and, in June 1860, joined with the Newport, Abergavenny & Hereford Railway and the Worcester & Hereford Railway (still being completed) to form the West Midland Railway. At the same time, permission was also gained to build a line from Stourbridge to Old Hill, the Stourbridge Railway, that would include branches to collieries and workshops. Further Parliamentary powers, the Stourbridge Extension Railway, extended the scheme to Galton Junction on the LNWR Birmingham to Wolverhampton line and to Handsworth on the GWR Birmingham to Wolverhampton route. Construction was complete by April 1863 to open the first two and a half miles to Cradley with an intermediate station at Lye and two goods branches were in operation by June. Construction continued to Old Hill, with final work completed to Galton Junction and Handsworth Junction on 1st April 1867. The WMR had already been absorbed by the GWR in 1863 so, of the two routes into Birmingham's centre, Stourbridge line trains found a natural home at Snow Hill, although the LNWR also ran services from New Street.

Trains to Stourbridge now added to the demands required of the original 1854 Snow Hill station, which had been deemed 'temporary' at its time of construction. Extra land was purchased at the western end of the site and the station rebuilt with enlarged facilities, opening in 1871. Now, there were two long, through platforms, with two through lines between, plus two bay platforms at the western end for terminating local trains. By the early 20th century, even this was inadequate, and further enlargement created a third Snow Hill that stood until demolition following withdrawal of its last trains in 1972.

Trains from Snow Hill took the Wolverhampton route through Birmingham's north-western suburbs that had stations at Hockley, Soho & Winson Green and Handsworth & Smethwick. Each station had extensive sidings with goods facilities, particularly at Hockley, where one of the three large sheds also covered canal wharfs. Various industries also connected to the route, several from sidings at Queens Head, near Handsworth, whilst, also in this area, was the Birmingham, Railway and Carriage Works that produced railway vehicles for home and export markets including early diesel trains and locomotives for British Railways. Through here, the railway climbed at gradients up to 1 in 90 and continued to do so after swinging southwards when leaving the Wolverhampton line at Handsworth Junction. Passing close by The Hawthorns stadium, home of West Bromwich Albion Football Club since 1900, platforms were provided from 1931 for fans on match days.

Shortly, the line arrived at Smethwick Junction station (later Smethwick West), after crossing deep canal cuttings, the LNWR Birmingham to Wolverhampton line and the junction for trains from New Street.

Leaving Smethwick, the line entered the Black Country. A commentator in the 1860s described this area as 'black by day and red at night', following his observations of industry smoke and furnace fires. Here were sidings, goods yards and branch lines connecting all kinds of industries to the railway and canal systems. The next stations originally were at Rood End and Oldbury & Langley Green, but these were replaced by a single station at Langley Green at the junction with a branch to Oldbury when that opened in 1885. For a short time this branch enjoyed a passenger service, but with several private sidings along the line and a large goods depot alongside the canal at its end, freight traffic was always going to be its raison d'être.

A falling gradient just before Rowley Regis & Blackheath station continued for the next three and a quarter miles through Old Hill and Cradley Heath & Cradley stations. This was Old Hill Bank, a notorious incline requiring extra locomotives to assist many climbing trains. Its prolonged gradients included 1 in 51 through Old Hill station and the 896-yard Old Hill Tunnel, where heat and exhaust from the leading locomotive could be choking for the crew working the rear one. Old Hill station itself was a junction. To the north, the Windmill End branch curved away to Dudley, along which was a branch to Withymoor Basin serving further collieries, furnaces and a canal basin. Southwards from here was the line to Halesowen, which served collieries and a canal basin before arriving at that station. The Halesowen Railway then continued under joint GWR and MR ownership to Longbridge on the MR Birmingham to Bristol main line, and this generated traffic to and from the Austin Motor Works after these opened in 1905.

Just before Cradley Heath & Cradley, the Corngreaves branch served several collieries and other industries as well as Cradley goods depot, reached by a track passing northwards under the Stourbridge line. At the station was another goods yard, within which was one of the connections with the Pensnett Railway. A final branch, the Hayes Lane branch, serving brickworks and more collieries, came just before Lye, whilst after Lye, the SR joined the original OWW line from Wolverhampton at Stourbridge Junction. Here, the original 1852 station was at the junction but, with enlargement of the railway yards in 1901, a new four-platform station was built to the south. This increase in facilities at Stourbridge was a measure of the importance of the town as a railway hub for the area, not only for the above industries but also for those along the OWW line northwards to Dudley and Wolverhampton. Another branch line joined at Stourbridge. This short, steeply graded line descended to a passenger station in the town and, later, was extended for goods trains to Amblecote canal basin and goods yard. Stourbridge factories generated their own trade, as the town was an important producer of glassware.

Leaving Stourbridge, the line became more rural in character as the Black Country was left behind. Stations at Hagley and Churchill and Blakedown served these villages, and after Hagley the line began a four and a half mile descent that included passing through the town of Kidderminster.

Here extensive goods facilities served the town's carpet trade, and south of the station was a junction to Bewdley for lines to Shrewsbury and Tenbury Wells. Along this branch, at Foley Park, was a sugar beet factory and other private sidings, all rail connected. Further south on the main line, the 371-yard Hoobrook Viaduct was originally built to Brunel's timber design but replaced by a brick structure during the mid-1880s. Another junction for Bewdley was at Hartlebury, this line

also serving Stourport-on-Severn, where coal trains were run to supply Stourport Power Station. Before reaching Droitwich (Droitwich Spa from 1923), sidings were provided at Elmley Lovett for War Department use and a small halt was provided at Cutnall Green. Just before Droitwich station, the line from Bromsgrove joined the route.

From here the five and a half mile run to Worcester passed a station at Fernhill Heath and extensive sidings and works at Blackpole. This latter site produced ordinance during both World Wars, and at other times cakes for Cadburys. Rainbow Hill Tunnel provided the entrance to Worcester, from where Shrub Hill station was reached by the line passing between railway workshops and locomotive sheds. Direct trains towards Hereford and south Wales left the route upon exiting the tunnel, whilst goods trains bypassed Shrub Hill using through sidings to the east of the station.

When the line first opened in 1867, passenger services consisted of seven trains each way from Snow Hill, with a similar number from New Street. At stations between Stourbridge and Worcester these also connected with existing OWW services between Wolverhampton and London Paddington. After 1917, the LNWR withdrew their service as a wartime economy measure, and this was not reinstated until 50 years later. The GWR developed services beyond Worcester to Malvern Wells, Hereford and Cardiff, with the Cardiff trains being advertised during the early 1900s as the *South Wales and Birmingham Express*. Summer excursion traffic also used the line, but Snow Hill to Stourbridge and Kidderminster was always an important Birmingham commuter route.

Branch lines added to the interest and complexity, but each fared differently with their passenger traffic. The Oldbury branch that had enjoyed 16 daily return trips in 1901 closed in 1915 as another casualty of World War I and never resumed. At Old Hill, the Halesowen branch was served by 15 trains per weekday in 1901, with some extended to Rubery via the Halesowen Railway. However, whilst this traffic officially ceased in 1927, unadvertised trains continued to run to Longbridge for Austin factory workers until 1958. The Old Hill to Dudley branch enjoyed a full service up to closure in 1964. At Stourbridge, the 'Town Car' traversed the steeply graded, double-track line to Stourbridge Town, a service which survives to this day. At Kidderminster, final trains ran to Bewdley and Stourport-on-Severn in 1970, the Wyre Forest and Severn valley lines from there having already closed in 1962 and 1963 respectively.

The role of Stourbridge as a freight hub has already been mentioned. Connecting with the Black Country's many sidings and yards were Bank Train locomotives, each being assigned specific duties at each location, tripping wagons to and from Stourbridge throughout the day when required. Timetabled freight trains connected Stourbridge with yards in Birmingham (Bordesley) and Wolverhampton (Oxley), and through trains called en-route to exchange wagons. In addition, Round Oak steelworks on the Wolverhampton line generated its own traffic. A fuel oil depot at Rowley Regis received trains from various refineries and others passed through to serve the oil depot at Soho Pool in Birmingham. A daily train used the Halesowen Railway to deliver Austin components from Oxford to Longbridge and, after this line's closure, the service transferred to the Bromsgrove route. Into the 1960s and Working Timetables were still scheduling such workings, but this was about to change. Cheaper and more flexible road transport, coupled with industry closures, was causing goods traffic to diminish, with most yards and sidings closing during the years 1964 and 1965. Those along the Wolverhampton route out of Snow Hill lasted a couple of years longer and the Halesowen branch continued to the end of that decade. Steam traction was also coming to the end of its reign, with Kidderminster depot closing in August 1964, Worcester depot by the end of 1965 and Stourbridge Junction in July 1966. Round Oak steelworks closed in 1982, but the site retains a steel terminal, receiving trains several times a day from south Wales. At Hartlebury, coal trains to Stourport Power Station ran until 1979, and Droitwich Spa's coal yard lasted until 1989. At Kidderminster, freight to the sugar beet works and private sidings continued until 1982. However, since then, this yard has been totally transformed into an impressive terminus for the Severn Valley Railway's heritage trains to Bewdley and Bridgnorth, opening in 1984.

Birmingham's passenger railway map was also changing. With the electrification of the West Coast main line and the rebuilding of New Street station in the mid-1960s, British Rail decided to concentrate all services on the rebuilt station. Stourbridge line trains switched to New Street from 6th March 1967, although a residual service to Langley Green was retained until 1972. Snow Hill station was demolished in the mid-1970s and the area left to wasteland. For a few years, the service from New Street was cut back to Kidderminster, but restoration to Worcester came in 1983. Another change of heart saw a new Snow Hill rise, first to serve Birmingham's southeast in 1987 and, eight years later, resumption of services to Smethwick and the Stourbridge line. Once again, Snow Hill has a cross-city service, having frequent trains between stations on the Worcester line towards Leamington Spa and Stratford-upon-Avon. Services are well patronised, and the future is looking bright for the modern Snow Hill to Worcester route.

BIRMINGHAM SNOW HILL

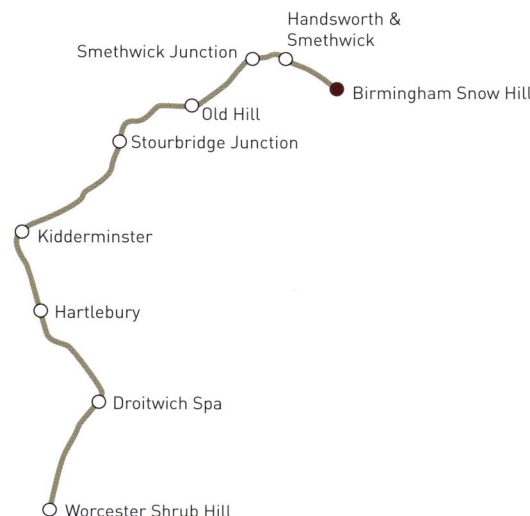

5101 class 2-6-2T No 4175 is starting away from Snow Hill platform 4 with an evening local to Stourbridge on 17th July 1965. These ex-GWR tank locomotives hauling rakes of suburban compartment coaches were commonplace on the route up to replacement by diesel trains, which were introduced from the late 1950s. An example of the latter is further back along platform 3. By the mid-1960s only a few peak-hour trains had retained steam-age configuration. In this view, locomotive numberplates have been replaced by painted and chalked numbers, indicating steam's imminent demise; withdrawal for No 4175 came in the following October from Stourbridge Junction shed.

For the first three miles, Worcester route trains shared tracks with services on the busy Wolverhampton main line. Here, a King class 4-6-0 is arriving at Snow Hill station with the Up *Cambrian Coast Express* during the latter days of steam working. This prestige train connected Welsh coastal towns between Pwllheli and Aberystwyth with London Paddington and has a uniform rake of the latest BR Mark 1 coaches, all painted in the former GWR chocolate and cream livery. The tall structure to the left of the photograph is Birmingham Snow Hill North signal box, built as such due to the site's confined space. Signals and points were electrically operated and powered by its own sub-station, plus battery back-up.

Around 30 years earlier, 3521 class 4-4-0 No 3555 is arriving hauling its train of suburban coaches. These locomotives were built as 0-4-2Ts in the late 1880s, with some, including this example, as saddle tanks for the Cornish broad-gauge lines. Rough riding caused all to be rebuilt as standard-gauge 0-4-4Ts but, without the issue solved, the GWR took the radical step of reversing the boiler to produce these 4-4-0 machines. Now as useful locomotives, most lasted until the late 1920s/early 30s. Running with a small tender, which enabled it to be turned on Kidderminster's short turntable, this locomotive was withdrawn in September 1929.

Perfectly framed between the North signal box and the twin spires of St Chad's Cathedral, Pannier tank 0-6-0 No 4646 has passed through Snow Hill station with a Down freight on 21st March 1960. With the locomotive being one of Stourbridge Junction's fleet at the time, this is likely to be one of the Bordesley to Stourbridge freights that were timetabled to run several times a day.

The first station out of Snow Hill was Hockley. Here, an engineer's train headed by 0-6-0 No 49 is passing in February 1911. This interesting locomotive dated from the earliest years of the OWW, being built by the Leeds firm of E. B. Wilson as OWW No 43 in 1856. First renumbered 264 upon absorption into the GWR stock, she underwent several rebuilds before withdrawal in 1921, a service life of 65 years.

HANDSWORTH & SMETHWICK

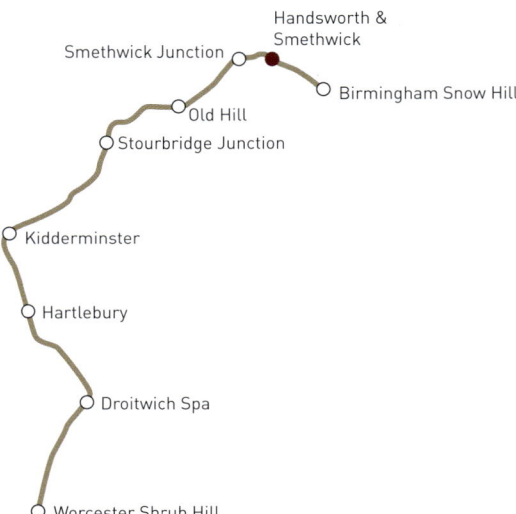

Passing Handsworth & Smethwick station with an empty train is 6100 class 2-6-2T No 6105. The spacious nature of this station is evident, as were the facilities at Hockley and Soho & Winson Green stations. To the east of this station were Queens Head sidings that included a cement terminal and scrap yard and, to the west, the Birmingham Railway and Carriage Works. As mentioned in the introduction, this firm was an important manufacturer of railway vehicles but added aircraft construction during the First World War and tanks and gliders during the Second.

The Worcester route left the main line at Handsworth Junction. In this view, GWR 4-4-4T No 27 joins the main line with a stopping train for Birmingham Snow Hill at some time in the 1920s. This was one of two similar locomotives built by Sharp Stewart in 1897 for the Midland & South Western Junction Railway and was their No 18. This was a cross-country route operating trains between Cheltenham Spa and Southampton but was absorbed into the GWR in 1923. Those locomotives not scrapped were re-numbered and No 27 has also been rebuilt with a standard GWR boiler and other features. Many ex-M&SWJR locomotives stayed near to their original route but this locomotive migrated to Kidderminster depot for local services until withdrawn from service in September 1929.

24 Lost Lines of England

SMETHWICK JUNCTION

An undated view of the junction and signal box at Smethwick Junction. The Stourbridge to Snow Hill line curves across the photograph between bottom right and centre left, whilst the approaching train is using the spur from the ex-LNWR line at Galton Junction. Unusually, coming from Birmingham's New Street station, this local train is headed by a Western Region 9400 class tank locomotive. After the Snow Hill lines were closed in 1972, a single track was retained from here to serve businesses at Queens Head sidings in Handsworth, but access from Snow Hill was re-established during the 1994 reconstruction of the route.

8100 class 2-6-2T No 8108 is arriving at Smethwick Junction station with a local train on 27th March 1951. Five years later the station was re-named Smethwick West and continued in use until 1996, after construction of the new station at Smethwick Galton Bridge. This latter facility, built where the Snow Hill line crossed the New Street route, provided a new interchange opportunity that gave an alternative to walking through Birmingham's city centre. After closure, Smethwick West station was stripped of buildings and facilities but its platforms have remained as a stark reminder of its former presence.

Upon opening the line in 1867 the next stations were Rood End and Oldbury & Langley Green. When the Oldbury branch opened in 1885 with a passenger service, both stations were closed and replaced by a new Langley Green station at the branch junction.

Between the original stations were Rood End sidings serving local industries, businesses along the Oldbury branch and, latterly, an oil depot at Rowley Regis. Here, Pannier tank 0-6-0 No 3619 is spending some quiet moments in the sidings on 19th September 1964.

When the Oldbury branch passenger service was closed in 1915, Langley Green station was renamed Oldbury & Langley Green. Approaching the station on 24th March 1957 is Modified Hall class 4-6-0 No 7918 *Rhose Wood Hall* hauling the 11.50 am (Sundays only) Birmingham Snow Hill to Cardiff train. Apart from special workings or route diversions, this was the only timetabled, long-distance passenger service to use the route. In the foreground are tracks to the freight-only Oldbury branch whilst the skyline is dominated by one of the Black Country's foundry buildings.

OLD HILL

The steep, 3¼-mile Old Hill Bank raises the line about 240 feet from the River Stour valley to the West Midlands plateau at gradients as steep as 1 in 51. Extra locomotives were stationed at Stourbridge to assist trains, either by attaching to the train locomotive at the front or as banking assistance in the rear. Here, with wide views across the Black Country landscape, the latter is the case, with two Pannier tanks climbing the gradient approaching Old Hill station. Curving away to the right is the branch to Blowers Green and Dudley, which served collieries, industries and canal basins before closure in 1964.

Birmingham to Worcester 31

Calling at Old Hill station on 27th March 1954 is the 4.23 pm Stourbridge Junction to Snow Hill, hauled by 5600 class 0-6-2T No 6698 and 8100 class 2-6-2T No 8101. The 2-6-2T would normally handle this train on its own, but, on this occasion, extra carriages have been added to accommodate fans attending a West Bromwich Albion football match at The Hawthorns stadium. No 6698 has been attached to assist with the climb.

The Halesowen branch was served by its own platform. Here, 7400 class 0-6-0PT No 7435 has arrived at the water tank with a train from Longbridge, probably in the late 1940s. Alongside, arriving at the Down main line platform, is an ex-GWR diesel railcar. Whilst 5700 class Pannier tanks could work on the branch as far as Halesowen, only lighter locomotives, such as the 7400 class, could work further due to a weight restriction over Dowry Dell Viaduct.

STOURBRIDGE JUNCTION

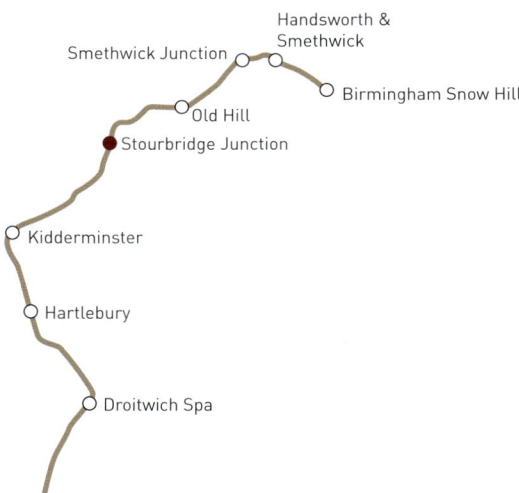

Handsworth & Smethwick
Smethwick Junction
Birmingham Snow Hill
Old Hill
Stourbridge Junction
Kidderminster
Hartlebury
Droitwich Spa
Worcester Shrub Hill

Leaving Stourbridge Junction for Birmingham Snow Hill is 3901 class 2-6-2T No 3920 with its smart train of clerestory vehicles. This class of 20 locomotives were converted from an 1896 batch of Dean Goods 0-6-0s for service with West Midlands local trains. They ran successfully here until the 1930s, when they were replaced by the 5100 class family of 2-6-2T locomotives. This particular locomotive, converted from 0-6-0 No 2502 in January 1910, was withdrawn from service in February 1931.

Birmingham to Worcester

5101 class 2-6-2T No 4158 has arrived at Stourbridge Junction platform 4 with a terminating train from Birmingham on 19th September 1964. The fireman has just removed a headlamp to transfer to a rear bracket for the locomotive to run round the train. This platform has since closed and, with the loss of local freight facilities, the land as far as the boundary fence has been redeveloped as the station car park.

Approaching Stourbridge Junction station is the autotrain from Stourbridge Town being propelled by an 0-4-2T locomotive. The driver can be seen in the coach's cab adjusting the speed of the train into the platform whilst the fireman keeps a sharp lookout from the locomotive's cab. This is teamwork in action as both men need to work together to safely work the train. This steep double-track branch was ultimately worked as two single lines, one passenger and the other freight, with the latter dropping further into Amblecote goods yard. Although the freight track to the right of the train was closed in 1965, the passenger service still operates using modern traction.

Birmingham to Worcester 39

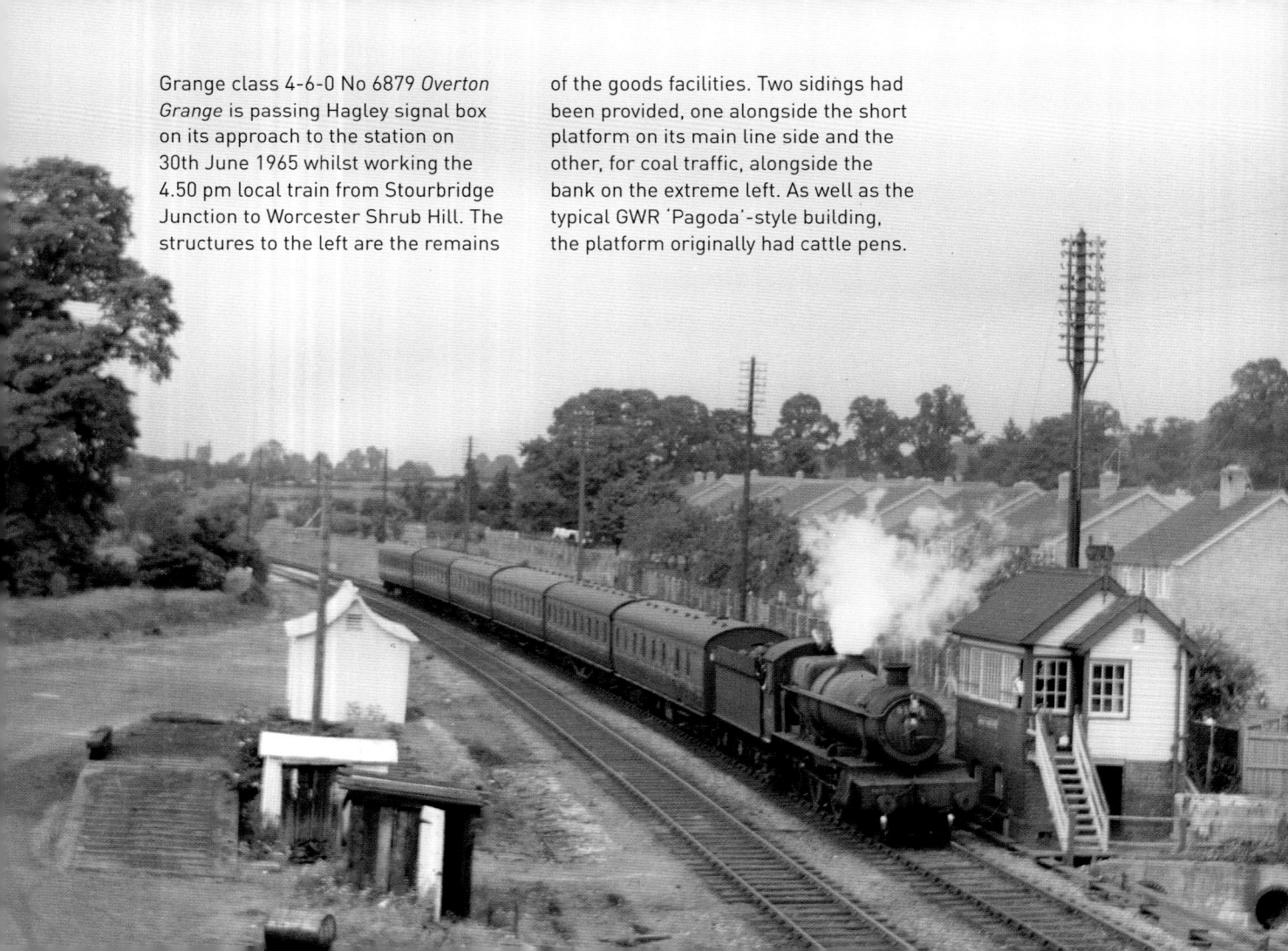

Grange class 4-6-0 No 6879 *Overton Grange* is passing Hagley signal box on its approach to the station on 30th June 1965 whilst working the 4.50 pm local train from Stourbridge Junction to Worcester Shrub Hill. The structures to the left are the remains of the goods facilities. Two sidings had been provided, one alongside the short platform on its main line side and the other, for coal traffic, alongside the bank on the extreme left. As well as the typical GWR 'Pagoda'-style building, the platform originally had cattle pens.

This is Churchill and Blakedown, the other intermediate station between Stourbridge Junction and Kidderminster. Seen in the distance on the other side of the level crossing are the goods facilities, which have the luxury of a brick-built goods shed and are clearly a step up from those at Hagley. As opposed to locations north of Stourbridge, freight traffic here was more typical of its rural landscape. At both here and Hagley, goods facilities were withdrawn on 1st February 1965, although passenger services still call.

KIDDERMINSTER

A busy scene at Kidderminster in late Victorian or Edwardian times. An Armstrong 'Standard Goods' 0-6-0 has drawn its train into the Up platform whilst, on the Down line, a horse is shunting a freight wagon. The track gang will have to move away for the horse to pass, but the signalman is keeping an eye on the proceedings from his signal box window. Kidderminster Station Signal Box, seen here, was commissioned in 1882 and its protection from any 'heavy shunt' in the siding appears only to be some sleepers across the rails.

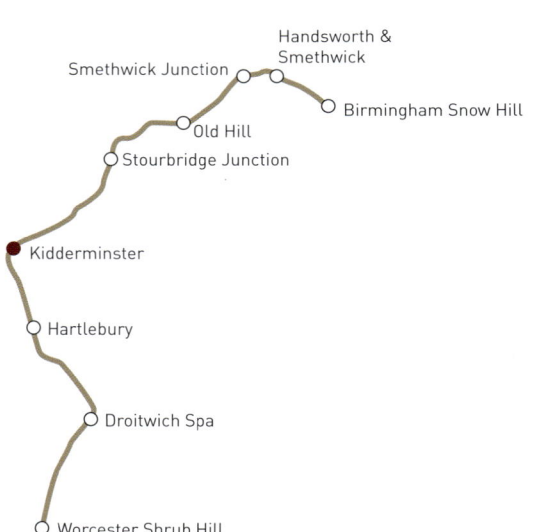

Ex-LNWR Class 7F 0-8-0 No 49108 has charge of a coal train for Stourport Power Station as it passes Kidderminster Up distant signal on 13th August 1954. These venerable locomotives were not uncommon on such trains, as much of the coal for this power station came from the coalfield at Cannock, this particular locomotive being allocated to Rycroft (Walsall) shed at the time. On arrival at Hartlebury, the wagons would be taken to Stourport by a local locomotive whilst the incomer used the Hartlebury-Bewdley-Kidderminster triangle to turn before collecting empties to take north.

2884 class 2-8-0 No 3800 has charge of a northbound freight near Kidderminster on 5th October 1962. In this direction, trains faced a rising gradient as far as Hagley, so the fireman will have been busy building the fire. However, in this view the boiler has steam to spare, so perhaps the fireman has been too keen or maybe the driver is now coasting towards unexpected adverse signals. The fitment in the opposite track is one of the GWR Automatic Train Control apparatus (ATC) ramps, an important safety system that gave drivers advance information about the next signal aspect. BR developed a similar system to a different design that is still in use today, the Automatic Warning System (AWS).

A busy scene south of Kidderminster station on 18th June 1953 sees Star class 4-6-0 4053 *Princess Alexandra* leaving with the 8.18 am Wolverhampton Low Level to Oxford and 2-6-0 No 6396 arriving with the morning Worcester to Kidderminster freight. The busy goods yard behind the trains closed in 1983, which allowed the Severn Valley Railway to develop its Kidderminster terminus on the site. Structures retained by the SVR, and here partially hidden by 4053's exhaust, are the goods shed and water tower. The goods shed was built exceptionally large to accommodate the town's flourishing carpet trade and is now home to the SVR's carriage maintenance workshops.

A wide view of the southern section of Kidderminster goods yard taken from the same footbridge, showing the long storage roads and several connections with the main line. In the distance, an ex-GWR diesel railcar is joining the main line from Bewdley and the signalman is walking out to collect the single line token. To the extreme right-hand side of the site, sand pits provided foundry sand to ex-GWR workshops. The yard's closure allowed the SVR to lay tracks to reach its new terminus, and a diesel depot and large carriage storage shed also now occupy the site.

HARTLEBURY

Manor class No 7802 *Bradley Manor* stands in Hartlebury station with the evening parcels train to Crewe on 9th October 1965. Station staff are loading the train further down the platform. Parcel trains were an integral part of the Post Office's delivery network, with timetabled services on all the major routes. Without name or numberplates, the locomotive is almost at the end of its main line life and was withdrawn from Shrewsbury depot a month later. However, after a number of years languishing in a south Wales scrapyard, she was bought and restored to service, now being one of the Severn Valley Railway's fleet. Just north of this station was Hartlebury Junction, where the line to Stourport, Bewdley and the Severn Valley diverged.

DROITWICH SPA

BR Standard class 5 4-6-0 No 73014 captures attention as it leads a train into Droitwich Spa from the Bromsgrove direction around 1951, a few months after the locomotive was built. She was allocated to Sheffield Millhouses depot, so is possibly working one of the daily through workings from her home town via Birmingham New Street towards the South West.

Just arrived in Droitwich Spa's Up platform is 5101 class 2-6-2T No 4147 with its two-coach local train. These locomotives dated from a prototype built in 1903, but more were built to updated designs from the late 1920s. As such, they became the GWR's standard locomotive for local and suburban passenger work. Batches were built at Swindon Works up to 1949, with No 4147 being a September 1946 product. She was withdrawn in October 1965, giving a service life of just over 19 years.

Former London Midland & Scottish Railway class 8F 2-8-0 No 48697 has charge of a southbound freight through Droitwich Spa station around 1965. This LMS standard goods locomotive was introduced in 1935 but production increased during World War II to 852 locomotives. Many were sent overseas for the war effort, although not this example. This locomotive was built in April 1944 at Brighton Works and saw service in the northwest of England, mostly based around Chester and Wrexham depots. Ex-GWR West Midlands rail routes were transferred from British Railway's Western Region to their London Midland region at the start of 1963, producing a new regional boundary on the Worcester line at Cutnall Green. Many ex-GWR locomotives working in the area were then gradually replaced by ex-LMS equivalents before steam working was abandoned in 1966.

WORCESTER SHRUB HILL

The prestige express to London Paddington was the *Cathedrals Express*. Here, its front portion from Kidderminster is approaching Shrub Hill station behind an unrecorded 2-6-2T. This curving approach passed between the railway works buildings on the extreme right and the locomotive sheds to the left, partly hidden behind the train. The rear portion from Hereford has already arrived behind a Modified Hall class locomotive and can be seen waiting at its signal towards the left of the photograph. Upon the front portion coming to a stand in the platform, a 'Calling On' signal would allow the rear portion to draw into the station for the attachment to take place.

58 Lost Lines of England

The Hereford portion of a London Paddington express has arrived at Worcester Shrub Hill behind Modified Hall class 4-6-0 No 7928 *Wolf Hall*. The wheeltapper is making his way down the train whilst the locomotive is using the scissors crossover to vacate the platform for the front portion, already further along the platform, to set back to complete the train. A Castle class 4-6-0 locomotive would normally take the combined train forward to London. In the near platform stands a Swindon-built diesel train working a Hereford and Cardiff line service. In the distance, glimpsed between the trains, are locomotives stabled at the locomotive shed.

From just after its opening in 1850 to nationalisation in 1948, trains from two rival companies used Shrub Hill station, which became jointly managed. Since 1923, after various mergers and takeovers, these companies had been the GWR and LMS. Here, LMS class 4P compound 4-4-0 No 1073 waits at the station with a stopping train for Birmingham New Street via Bromsgrove circa 1941. The station not only served such stopping and semi-fast services originating from Birmingham New Street but also longer-distance trains from the East Midlands and North East to Bristol and the South West, with extra trains calling on Saturdays during the summer holiday season.

CREDITS

Lost Lines of England – Birmingham to Worcester

Published in Great Britain in 2025 by Graffeg Limited.

ISBN 9781802583489

Text by Roger Norfolk copyright © 2025. Designed and produced by Graffeg Limited copyright © 2025.

Graffeg Limited, 15 Neptune Court, Vanguard Way, Cardiff, CF24 5PJ, Wales, UK. Tel: 01554 824000. croeso@graffeg.com. www.graffeg.com.

Roger Norfolk is hereby identified as the author of this work in accordance with section 77 of the Copyright, Designs and Patents Act 1988.

Printed by 1010 Printing, China.

A CIP Catalogue record for this book is available from the British Library.

All rights reserved. No part of this publication may be reproduced, stored in a retrieval system or transmitted, in any form or by any means, electronic, mechanical, photocopying, recording or otherwise, without the prior permission of the publishers.

This book is designed for general readers, printed with materials and processes that are safe and meet all applicable European safety requirements. The book does not contain elements that could pose health or safety risks under normal and intended use.

We hereby declare that this product complies with all applicable requirements of the General Product Safety Regulation (GPSR) and any other relevant EU legislation.

Appointed EU Representative:
Easy Access System Europe Oü, 16879218
Mustamäe tee 50, 10621, Tallinn, Estonia
gpsr.requests@easproject.com

1 2 3 4 5 6 7 8 9

Photo credits

© Kidderminster Railway Museum: cover and pages 25, 33, 34, 43, 45, 63.

© Kidderminster Railway Museum/ W Potter: page 17. © Kidderminster Railway Museum/H W Burman: page 21. © Kidderminster Railway Museum/J Wood: pages 27, 32.

© Kidderminster Railway Museum/J Richards: page 29. © Kidderminster Railway Museum/B Moone: pages 40, 44, 47. © Kidderminster Railway Museum/P Riley: page 50. © Kidderminster Railway Museum/J D Mills: page 52. © Kidderminster Railway Museum/J Tarrant: page 56. © Great Western Trust: pages 30, 38, 41, 48.

© Roger Norfolk: pages 12, 28, 36.
© Transport Treasury: page 26.
© Transport Treasury/R C Riley: pages 15, 18.
© Transport Treasury/N Stead: pages 22, 61.
© Transport Treasury/J Harrold: page 55.
© Transport Treasury/Milepost: page 59.

The photographs used in this book have come from a variety of sources. Wherever possible contributors have been identified although some images may have been used without credit or acknowledgement and if this is the case apologies are offered and full credit will be given in any future edition.

Cover: Kidderminster.
Back cover: Rood End Sidings, Stourbridge Junction, Birmingham Snow Hill.

Lost Tramways UK and Ireland series:

www.graffeg.com

Lost Lines of England:

Birmingham to Oxford ISBN 9781912654871
Birmingham to Worcester ISBN 9781802583489
Matlock to Buxton ISBN ISBN 9781802583472
Ryde to Cowes ISBN 9781912654864
Stratford-upon-Avon to Gloucester ISBN 9781802582024
The Cheddar Valley Line ISBN 9781913134402

Lost Lines of England and Wales:

Shrewsbury to Chester ISBN 9781914079122
Wye Valley ISBN 9781802582017

Lost Lines of Wales series:

Aberystwyth to Carmarthen ISBN 9781909823198
Bangor to Afon Wen ISBN 9781912213115
Brecon to Newport ISBN 9781909823181
Cambrian Coast Line ISBN 9781909823204
Chester to Holyhead ISBN 9781912050697
Conwy Valley Line ISBN 9781912654147
Llandovery to Craven Arms ISBN 9781914079115
Monmouthshire Eastern Valley ISBN 9781802581089
Monmouthshire Western Valley ISBN 9781802581102
Rhyl to Corwen ISBN 9781912213108
Ruabon to Barmouth ISBN 9781909823174
Shrewsbury to Aberystwyth ISBN 9781912050680
Swansea to Llandovery ISBN 9781914079108
The Heads of the Valleys Line ISBN 9781912654154
The Mid Wales Line ISBN 9781912050673
Vale of Neath ISBN 9781912050666

Scan the QR code to see the Lost Lines collection. Also eBooks available for Kindle and Apple Books.